Contents

Melbourn, Cambridgeshire 1954

Outside the home

Harlow, Essex 1957

Look at this photograph. The houses on the left are terraced houses.
Each one is joined to the house next door. The large building
on the right is divided into flats. Several families live in
this building.

Look for:

— the balconies in the flats
— the garages in a row, by the flats
— the trees and bushes
— the television aerials.

**"We lived in a new terraced house. The walls were not very thick.
We could hear someone playing the piano from two houses away."**

Look at this photograph of a new house. It was built over 30 years ago. The outside walls have plaster over the bricks.

Materials for building new houses were difficult to get in the early 1950s. Timber and steel were rationed.

"Bricks had to be ordered at least one year before you needed them."

Throckley, Northumberland 1951

Things to do

Start to make a book about life *At home in the 1950s.* Find some houses or flats near where you live that were built in the 1950s.
Draw a picture or take a photograph of them. Stick the picture in your book.

Talk to someone over 30 about the new houses that were built in the 1950s. Write down what they tell you.

Inside the home

Harlow, Essex 1955

**"We loved our new house. Everything was light and airy.
After living in a converted Nissen hut, it was marvellous
to be warm and dry."**

Look at this photograph of a sitting room.

Look for:

— the fireplace which burns coal
— the piano
— the armchairs which have wooden armrests and spaces in the frames.
  Furniture in the 1950s was lighter in colour and weighed less.
— the size and shape of the table legs
— the patterns on the vases. They were designed to go with
  the new furniture.
— the venetian blind at the window.

These plates were bought in the 1950s. Look at the leaf pattern.

Many new ideas for objects in the house were first shown at the 1951 Festival of Britain. This powder compact had face powder in it. Look for the date.

"I went on a school outing to the Festival of Britain in London. It was very exciting to see the new things that were being made."

Things to do

Draw a picture of your sitting room. Is the furniture in your room different or the same as the furniture in the photograph?

Ask an adult if they have objects in their home from the 1950s. Perhaps they will allow you to draw these objects. Write underneath your drawings anything they tell you about these things.

Radio

Most homes in the 1950s had a radio. It worked by having its plug put into an electric socket on the wall.

"If our radio ever went wrong, my Dad used to fix it. He'd take off the back. Inside were large metal things like upside down bottles called valves."

This is a picture of a radio called a wireless.

Look for:

— the four plastic knobs. These were used to switch the radio on and off. They were also used to find different programmes.
— the two speakers above the knobs where the sound came from
— the air vent at the side to stop the radio getting too hot inside.

Pye Fen Man radio 1955

6

This photograph shows
three men making a radio
programme.
Their programme was very
funny. It was called
"The Goon Show".
The men's names (from
left to right) are
Peter Sellers,
Harry Secombe and
Spike Milligan.

"The Goon Show", BBC Home Service 1960

"I never missed 'The Goon Show'.
My favourite person in the show was called Bluebottle.
I could copy his funny voice."

Things to do

Compare the size of the wireless with a transistor radio
in your home. Find out why your radio is smaller.

Ask an adult to tell you about their favourite radio programme
in the 1950s. How often did they listen to the radio?
Write down what they tell you.

Television

"We were so excited when we had our first telly. The picture was black and white. We watched everything. It was like going to the cinema every day."

A television set was an expensive item to buy. Most families did not have a television in their home in the early 1950s. It was something you might watch in a friend's home if they were wealthy enough to own a television. Later in the 1950s, more families bought television sets.

*Right:
Pye television
set 1949*

Christopher Trace and Leila Williams were the first presenters of a new children's television programme. It was called "Blue Peter".

**"I loved Muffin the Mule.
He was so sweet. I even had
a puppet exactly like Muffin.
It was a Christmas present."**

The puppet in this photograph became
a famous television character. He was
called Muffin the Mule. The woman at
the top made the puppet move by
pulling the strings. The other woman
talked to the puppet and played
the piano. Muffin danced on top of
the piano.

BBC television 1952

Things to do

Look carefully at the clothes worn by the presenters of "Blue Peter".
Do they look different from those worn by the people who present
"Blue Peter" now? Make a list of the differences in your book.

Draw a picture of Muffin the Mule. Then draw beside it a picture
of a puppet from a children's television programme today.

The kitchen

"It was the first time I had hot water from the tap."

Families wanted to have kitchens that were easy to use. New equipment was bought so that less time was spent on the jobs in the kitchen.

Refrigerators kept food fresh for a long time. Now shopping did not have to be done every day.

Olympia 1955

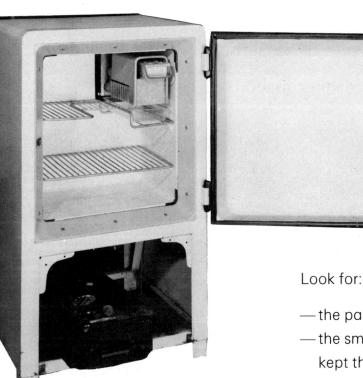

This type of refrigerator was made so that it could work on gas, electricity or paraffin. This one worked on paraffin.

Look carefully at the photograph.

Look for:

— the paraffin container at the bottom
— the small size of the part that kept the food cold
— the ice tray.

Electrolux refrigerator 1950

"If my fridge stopped working, I just tipped it on one side. I could hear the liquid moving around inside. Anyway, whatever it was I did, the fridge always started to work again."

Things to do

Make two lists in your book. Call one list *Kitchens then*. Write about kitchens and kitchen equipment in the 1950s. Call the other list *Kitchens now*. Write about kitchens today.

Washday

"My washing machine made the job of washing the clothes much easier. It was quicker too."

Look at the photograph of a woman washing a football team's kit. The washing machine is made of steel. Can you see the wringer on the top of the machine? The rollers squeezed the water out of the wet clothes.

Colchester, Essex 1950

Before the 1950s, washing machines had to be filled with water that was already hot. The washing machine in the photograph worked by electricity. Electric heaters were fitted to the washing tub. Cold water was put in the machine and heated by the electric heater.

12

1 Sort whites, coloureds, and woollens while filling the Parnall All-Electric Safety Washer by the flexible hose which will fit your hot-water tap. (There is a Parnall model that will boil the water too!)

2 Load Washer with clothes . . . and switch on . . .

3 Time for a "cuppa" while the Washer gently but thoroughly washes the clothes by unique Parnall "washing-swirl" action . . .

60 minute washday!

4 Reload the Washer with more dirty clothes and whilst these are being washed, rinse and wring the first load through the Parnall Safety Power Wringer . . .

5 Just one hour gone and a week's average family wash is out on the line . . . clean and fine. Then let the Parnall empty itself — by power.

PARNALL

ALL-ELECTRIC · World's Best Safety Washer

£65·2·0 TAX PAID—or with Water Heater **£75·12·0**
— *and really easy terms*

SEE ONE AT YOUR LOCAL DEALER'S OR ELECTRICITY SHOWROOMS

Parnall (Yate) Ltd., 255 North Circular Road, Neasden, London, N.W.10
WHG P.33

Advertisement 1955

This is an advertisement for a washing machine.

Look for:

— the time the makers claim it will take to do the washing
— the prices. Could you buy a new washing machine for that price today?

"I bent down to get the wet clothes out of the washing machine. My little girl thought she'd help. She started the power ringer and caught my hair in the rollers. It did hurt."

Things to do

Find out how much time a load of clothes takes to wash today. Write this time down. Compare this with the time in the advertisement.

Are your wet clothes hung on a line to dry?

Ask someone over 30 if they remember their first electric washing machine.

Boys' and girls' clothes

"Boys always wore short trousers. I didn't get my first long pair until I was thirteen. My knees got very sore and chapped during the winter."

These boys are playing a game called "Weak 'orses". How do you think it was played?

Look for:

— the length of the short trousers. Look at the length of the short trousers that boys wear now.
— the long woollen socks
— the overcoats
— the boots
— the boy's cap.

London

**"I used to spend
hours ironing
my daughter's
summer dresses.
It was really hard to
iron out the creases."**

Look at the photograph
of the three girls.
The girl in the middle
came from Jamaica.
Many West Indian
families came to Britain
to get work in the 1950s.

Brixton, London 1952

Look for:

— the girls' dresses. Do girls always wear dresses
  in the summer now?
— the canvas sandals worn by the girl on the left.
  They had to be cleaned with whitener.

Things to do

Ask an adult if they remember any of their favourite clothes that
they wore when they were your age. Ask them to describe these clothes.
Perhaps they could show you some photographs of themselves.

Draw a picture of a boy and a girl from the 1950s.

Toys, comics and books

"I played a great game. I was Davy Crockett with my fur hat. I would pretend to track my mates who were the Indians."

Many toys were based on characters in films and comics. This picture shows a boy dressed up in a Dan Dare space suit.

Below: London 1951

London 1954

This boy is playing with a toy horse. It was called a Mobo Horse. You sat on the saddle and pushed down. The horse would then move forwards.

"I had a baby doll. All it did was cry and blink its eyes."

Here are some comics and annuals
from the 1950s.

**"I had the 'Girls' Crystal' magazine each week and the annual each
Christmas. I loved the stories about schoolgirls in boarding schools."**

Look at some of these words that were used in comics and annuals:

"Wizard idea! Golly!"
"It was a silly jape."
"The cunning bounder."
"The chums rushed to the rescue."

Things to do

Talk to several adults. Ask them to tell you about their
favourite toys, comics and books. Make a list of them in your book.
Can you buy any of these comics or annuals now?

Visit your local museum. Find out if they have an old toys' exhibition.

Plastics

Plastic was used more and more in the home. It was easy to clean and it did not weigh much.

"I used to spend two hours putting on my make-up. I wanted to look glamorous."

"I used to buy Airspun Face Powder by Coty. It cost 5 shillings (25p). **My mum gave me a Toni Home Perm. The smell of the perm lotion was terrible."**

Look carefully at
the photograph of
a plastic make-up bag.

Look for:

— the plastic jars and
   bottle with screw-top
   lids
— the fluffy powder puff
— the quilted plastic
   material with a flower
   pattern on it.

**"I went dancing twice a week.
The new music was rock and roll."**

Plastic was used to make records.
More and more people bought records
in the 1950s.

Look again at page 10. Look for
the things made from plastic
in the kitchen.

Things to do

Ask an adult where they liked to go when they went out.
Did they enjoy dancing? What sort of music did they
listen to? Write down what they tell you in your book.

Listen to an old rock and roll record.

Collect items made of plastic that were made in the 1950s.

Coronation day

On 2 June 1953
Queen Elizabeth II
was crowned.
All over Britain,
people had their own
celebrations at home.
Some people had a
street party for
the children.

*Bethnal Green,
London 1953*

**"I ate so much cake and jelly that I made myself sick.
I had a red, white and blue paper hat. We had a huge
Union Jack hanging from my bedroom window."**

Look carefully at the photograph above of a street party.
Look at the number of men wearing suits. Look for the party hats
and the flags. Can you see any television aerials?

These children are singing and dancing. They are giving this performance to celebrate the Queen being crowned. These children lived in a street in London. People who lived there collected money for 10 months. Then they had enough money for a street party and entertainment.

London 1953

Things to do

Go to your local library. Find a book which has photographs of Queen Elizabeth II being crowned.

Ask several adults if a street party was held in their street to celebrate the Coronation. Find out if they own a special Coronation mug.

Imagine you were at a Coronation street party in 1953. Write about what happened.

Shopping

In the early 1950s, every member of a family had a food ration book. The shopkeeper used to cut out coupons from these books. This would allow each family to buy a certain amount of food. Even sweets were rationed.

"Shopping took hours. My feet used to ache from queuing. I was fed up with rationing."

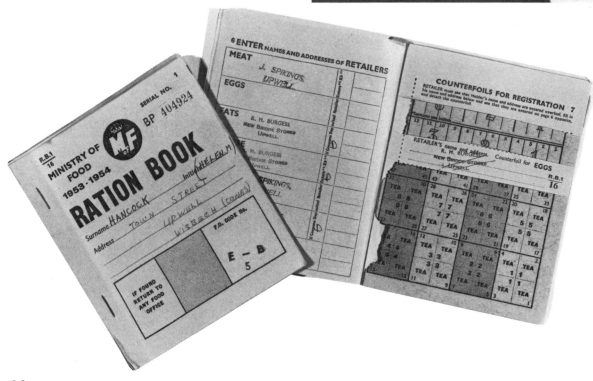

Harlow, Essex 1953

Look carefully at the photograph above. It shows a shopping centre in a new town.

Look for:

— the people queuing for bread
— the man wearing trousers that come down just below the knees. These are called "plus fours".
— the motor bike with side car
— the high pram
— the ladies wearing headscarves
— the long coats.

Things to do

Ask someone over 30 what they remember about shops and shopping when they were your age. Write down what you find out.

In 1952, each person was allowed 14 ounces (395 grams) of meat each week. The price of this was 1 shilling and 9 old pence (9p). Find out how much meat your family eats each week now. How much does your meat cost?

At home

This mother is busy knitting and her two daughters are looking at a book. Perhaps the mother has finished all her jobs in the house. Look at her headscarf. This was to keep her hair clean.

Harlow, Essex 1950

Would you have enjoyed living in a home like this in the 1950s?

Most towns have some housing estates that were built in the 1950s. Is there one near where you live?

The following New Towns were built in the 1950s. Some of them have museums.

Basildon, Essex
Bracknell, Berkshire
Corby, Northamptonshire
Crawley, Sussex
Cumbernauld, Strathclyde
Cwmbran, Gwent
East Kilbride, Strathclyde

Glenrothes, Fife
Harlow, Essex
Hatfield, Hertfordshire
Hemel Hempstead, Hertfordshire
Newton Aycliffe, County Durham
Peterlee, County Durham
Welwyn Garden City, Hertfordshire

Only a few of these towns have begun to collect photographs of their early history. Perhaps you can help by collecting photographs and objects yourself.